CONTENTS

Music transcriptions by Martin Shellard

ISBN 978-1-4234-8498-1

HAL•LEONARD®
CORPORATION
7777 W. BLUEMOUND RD. P.O. BOX 13819 MILWAUKEE, WI 53213

Visit Hal Leonard Online at
www.halleonard.com

Oblivion

Words and Music by Brann Dailor, William Hinds, William Kelliher and Troy Sanders

Drop D tuning, down 1 step:
(low to high) C-G-C-F

Intro
Moderately ♩ = 103

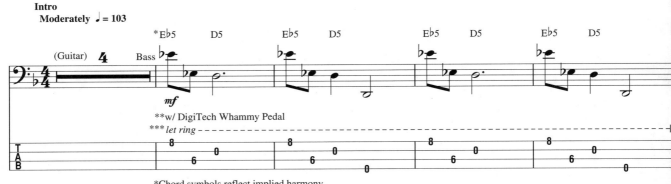

*Chord symbols reflect implied harmony.
**Set to detune.
***Applies to 2nd & 4th strings only.

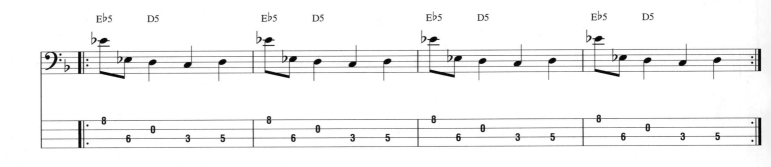

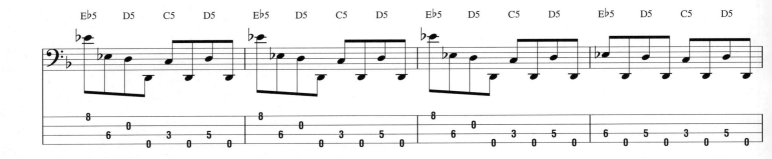

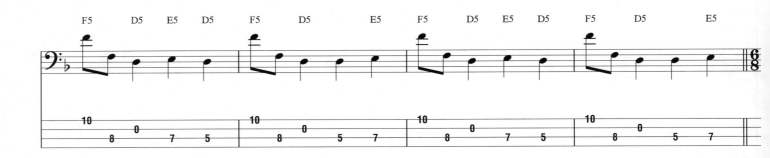

Fill 1
Bass

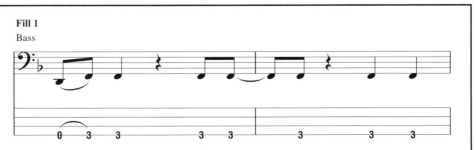

*3rd time, upstemmed vocal tacet.

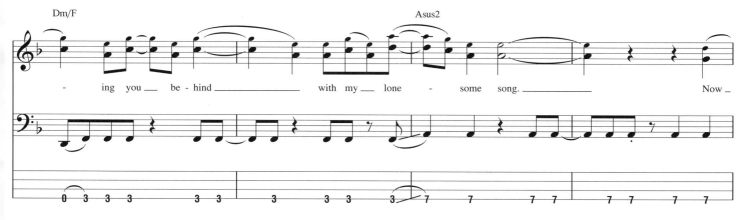

⊕ Coda 1

Fall - ing from _____ grace _____ 'cause I been a - way _____

_____ too long. _____ Leav - ing you _____ be - hind _____ with my _____ lone -

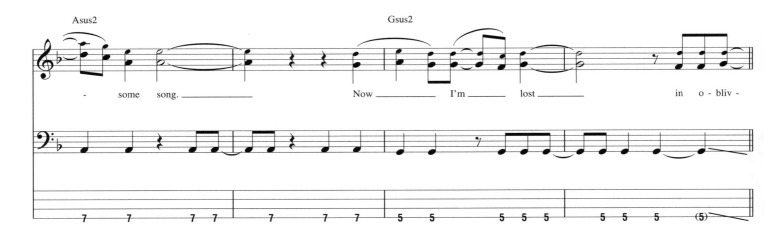

- some song. _____ Now _____ I'm _____ lost _____ in o - bliv -

Interlude

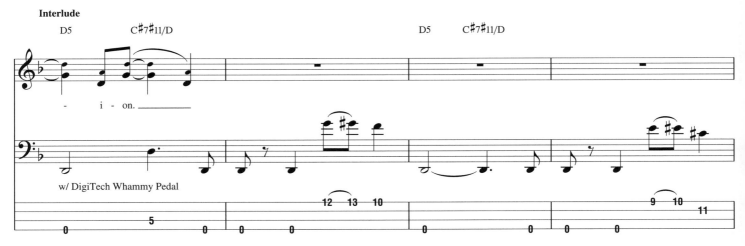

- i - on. _____

w/ DigiTech Whammy Pedal

6

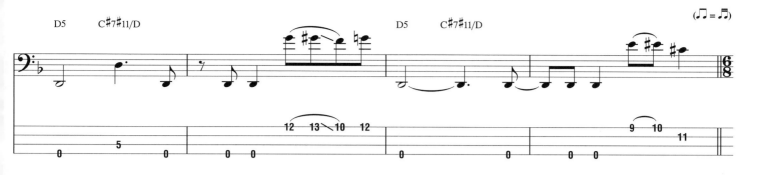

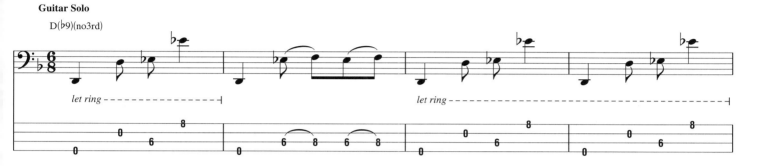

Guitar Solo

End half-time feel

7

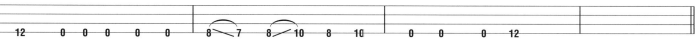

D.S.S. al Coda 2

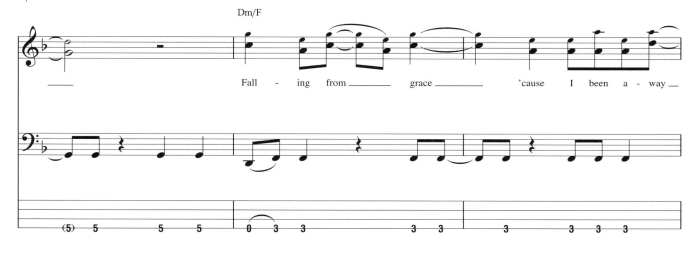

Coda 2

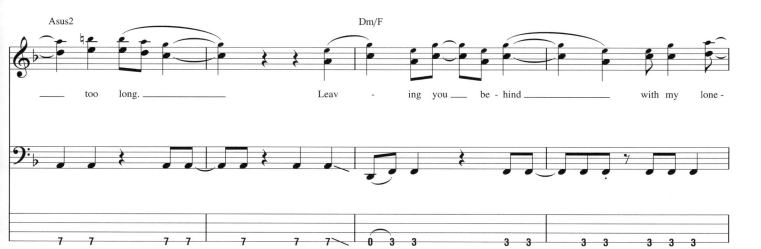

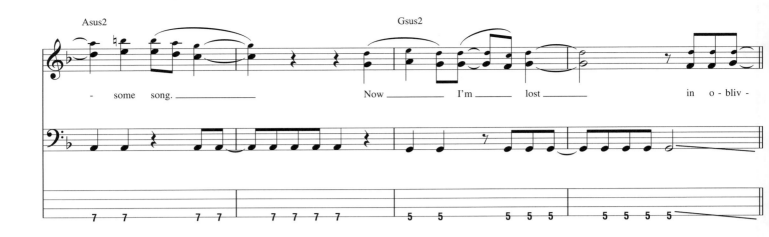

Outro

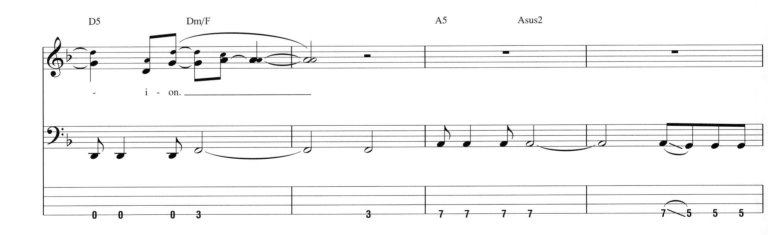

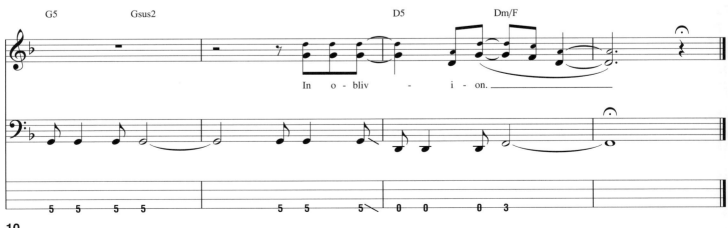

10

Divinations

Words and Music by Brann Dailor, William Hinds, William Kelliher and Troy Sanders

Tune down 1 step:
(low to high) D-G-C-F

Verse

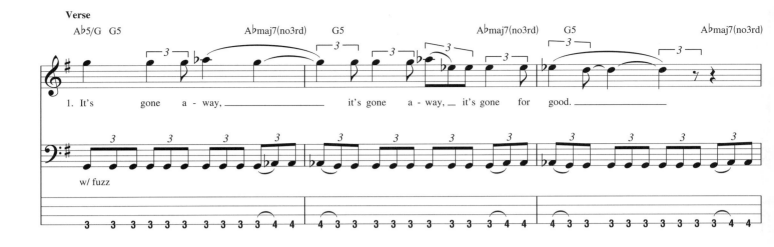

1. It's gone a - way, _____ it's gone a - way, _ it's gone for good. _____

w/ fuzz

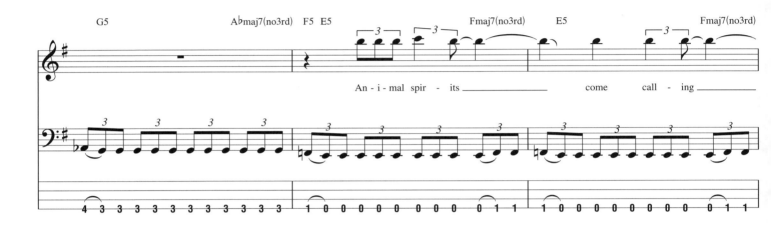

An - i - mal spir - its _____ come call - ing _____

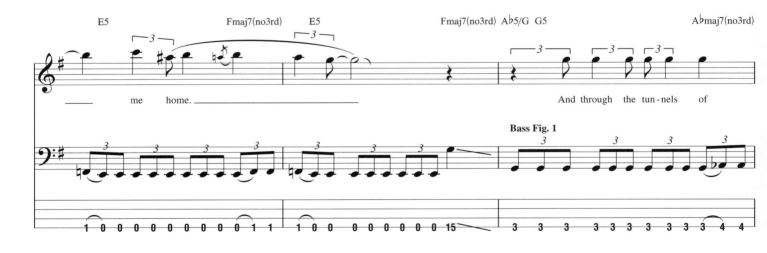

_____ me home. _____ And through the tun - nels of

Bass Fig. 1

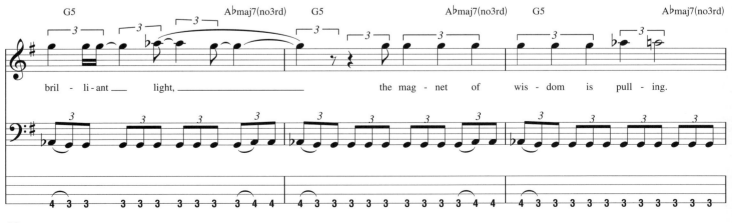

bril - li - ant _ light, _____ the mag - net of wis - dom is pull - ing.

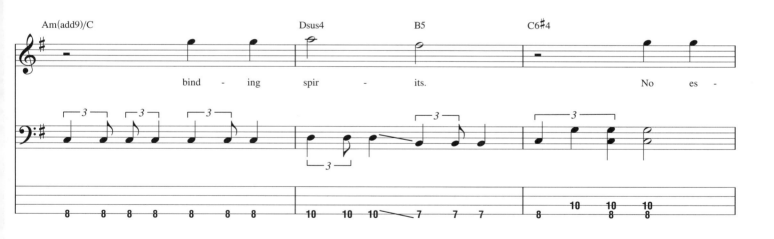

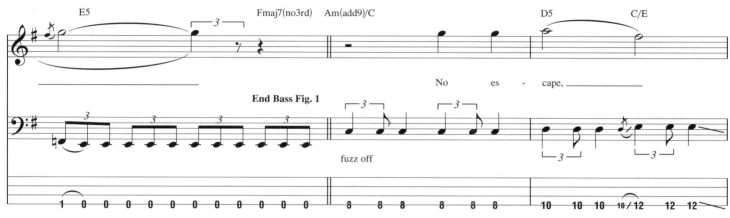

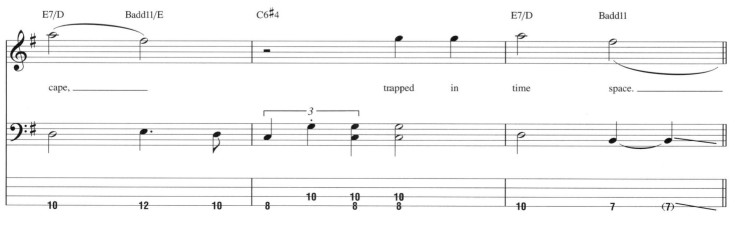

Verse

Bass: w/ Bass Fig. 1 (2 times)

2. Rap - id de - scen - dants, the worm - hole is emp - ty.

The cen - ter of Khl - ys - ty sur - rounds me.

The fire's danc - ing in a sil - ver - y sheet of breath.

Black robe, nec - ro - manc - ing, sum - mon the soul of the spec - tre.

Pre-Chorus

No es - cape, bind - ing spir - its.

Bass

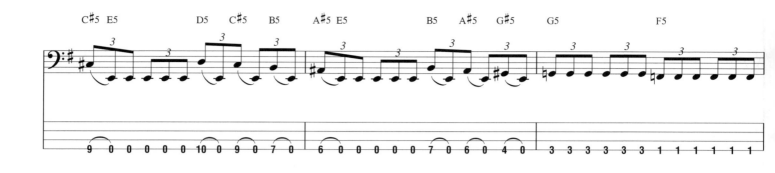

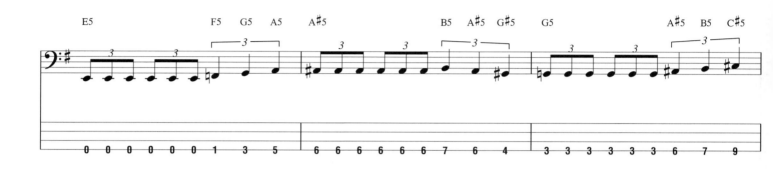

Guitar Solo
Bass: w/ Bass Fig. 2

Pre-Chorus

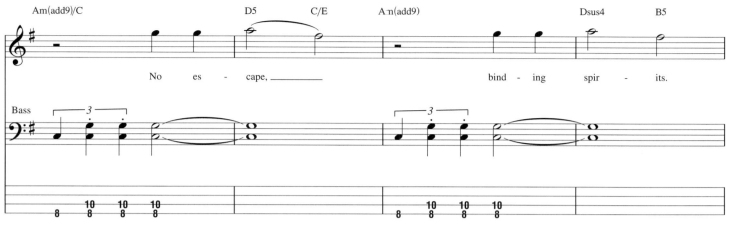

No es - cape, ____ bind - ing spir - its.

D.S. al Coda

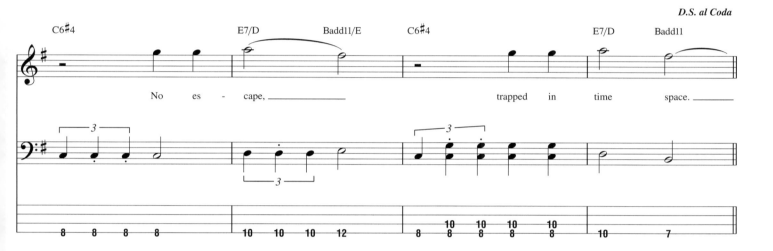

No es - cape, ____ trapped in time space. ____

⊕ **Coda**

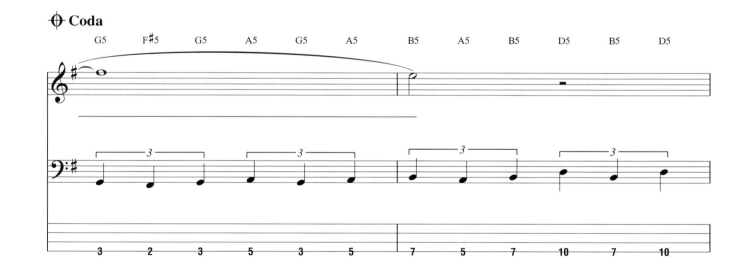

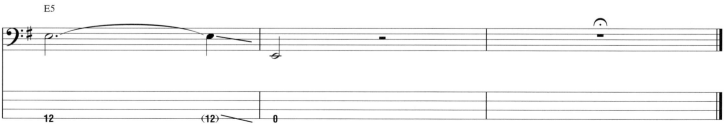

Quintessence

Words and Music by Brann Dailor, William Hinds, William Kelliher and Troy Sanders

Tune down 1 step:
(low to high) D-G-C-F

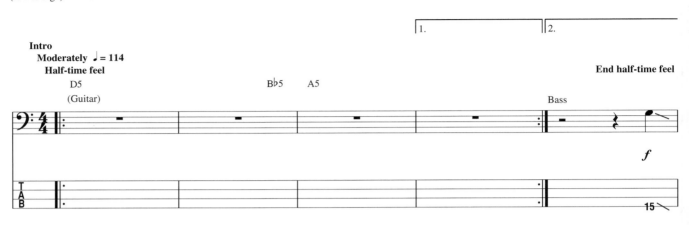

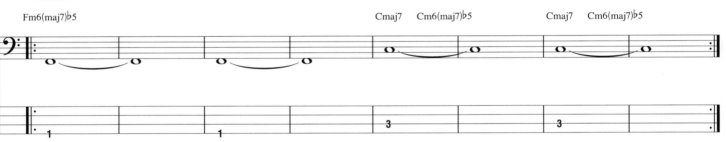

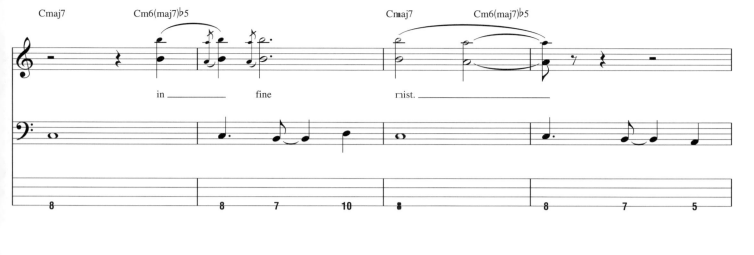

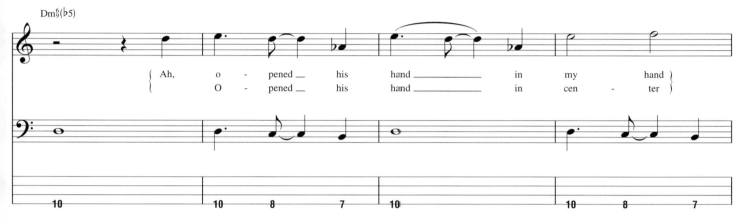

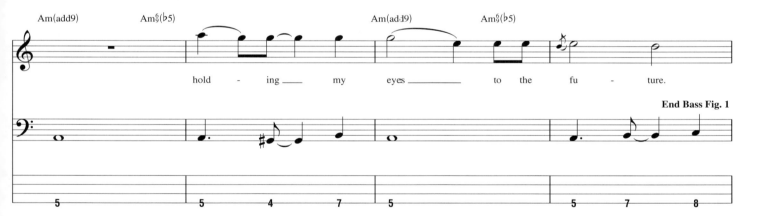

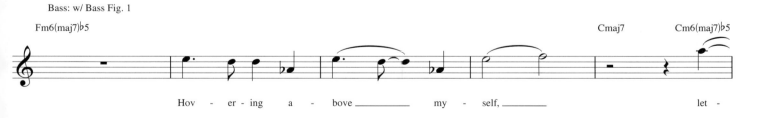

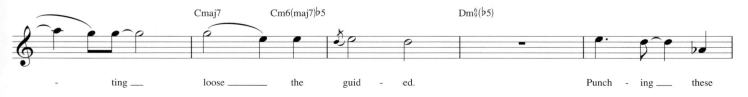

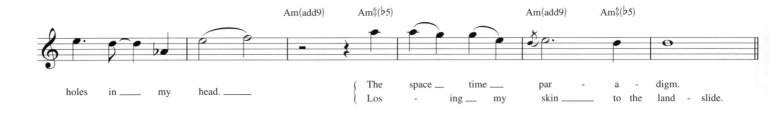

holes in ___ my head. ___

The space ___ time ___ par - a - digm.
Los - ing ___ my skin ___ to the land - slide.

Interlude

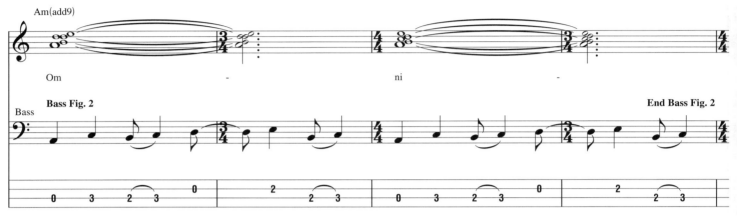

Om - ni -

Bass Fig. 2 **End Bass Fig. 2**

pres - ence. ___

Bass: w/ Bass Fig. 2

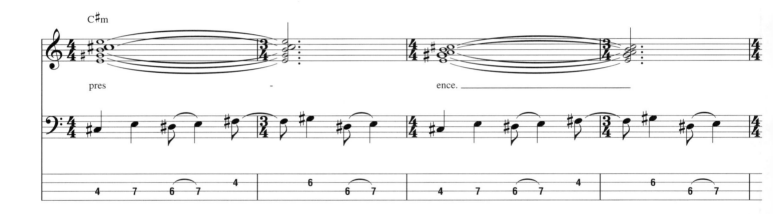

Pri - mal ___

in - stincts. ___

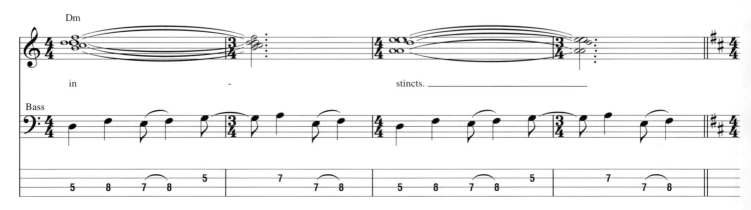

Pre-Chorus

Let it go, _____ let it go. _____

Let it go, _____ let it go. _____

(Let it go, _____ let it go.) _____

Chorus

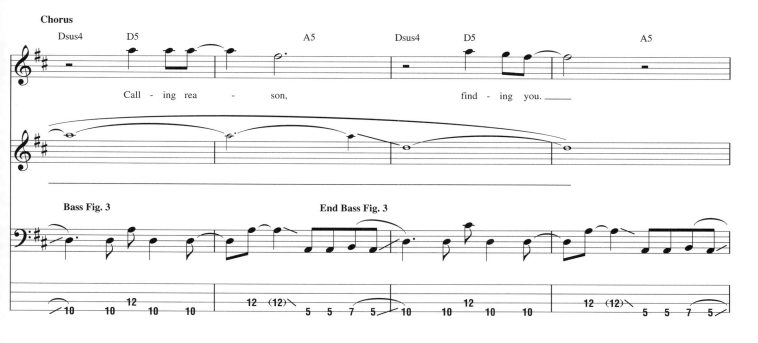

Call - ing rea - son, find - ing you. _____

Bass Fig. 3   **End Bass Fig. 3**

Bass: w/ Bass Fig. 3 (5 1/2 times)

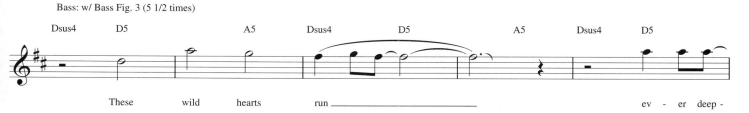

These wild hearts run _____ ev - er deep-

Outro

Half-time feel

Bass Fig. 4

Shield _____ fail - ure. _____

Speed _____ fare - well. _____

End Bass Fig. 4

The Czar

Words and Music by Brann Dailor, William Hinds, William Kelliher and Troy Sanders

Tune down 1 step:
(low to high) D-G-C-F

"Usurper"

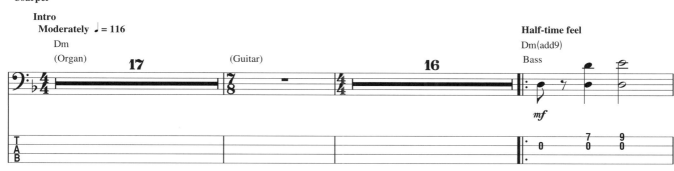

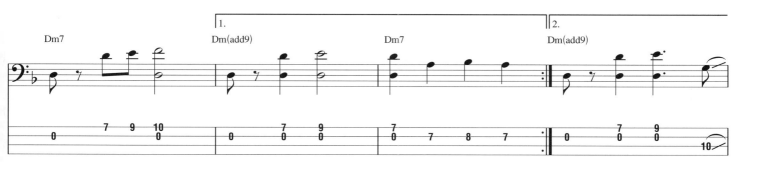

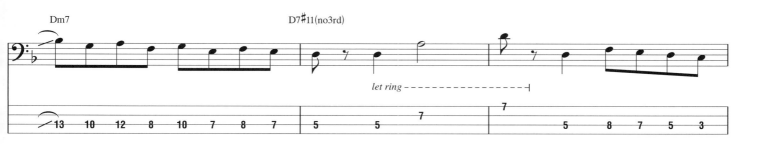

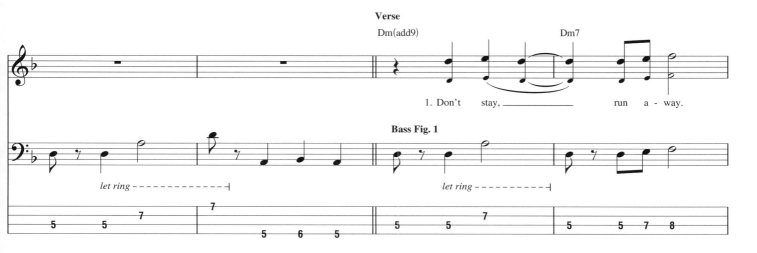

1. Don't stay, _____ run a way.

He has or-dered as-sas-si-na-tion. _____ Don't stay, _____ run a-way. _____

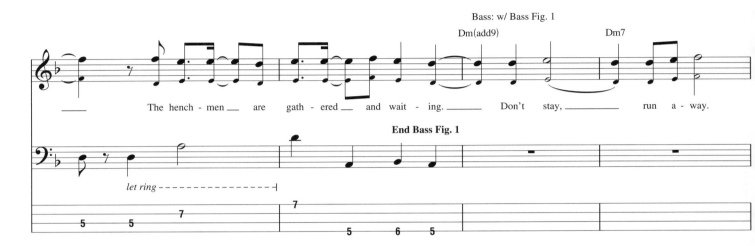

Bass: w/ Bass Fig. 1

_____ The hench-men _____ are gath-ered _____ and wait-ing. _____ Don't stay, _____ run a-way.

End Bass Fig. 1

Your role as _____ u-surp-er _____ is found _____ out. _____ Don't stay, _____

_____ run a-way. Tsar-i-na _____ has warned of _____ the dan-ger.

Interlude

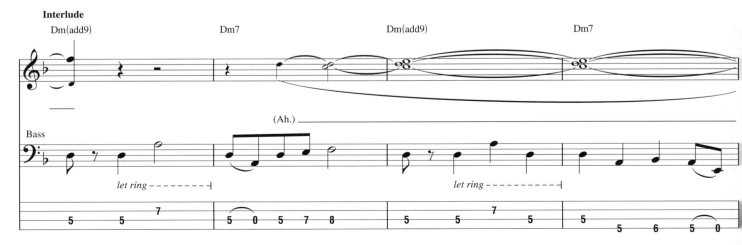

(Ah.) _____

Bass

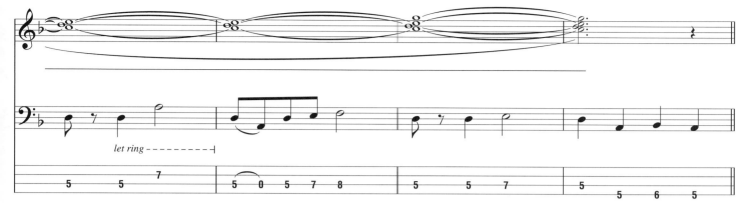

Chorus

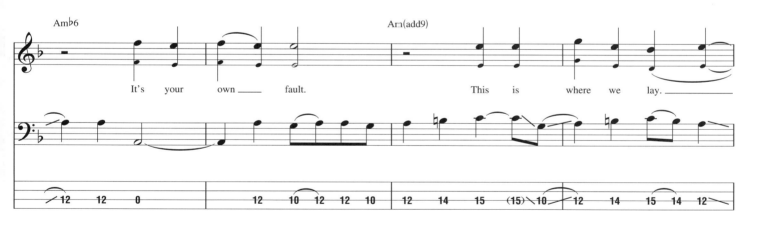

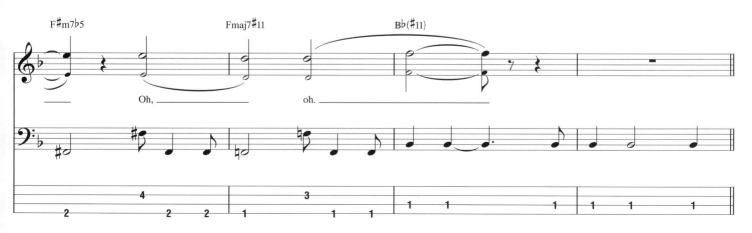

Verse

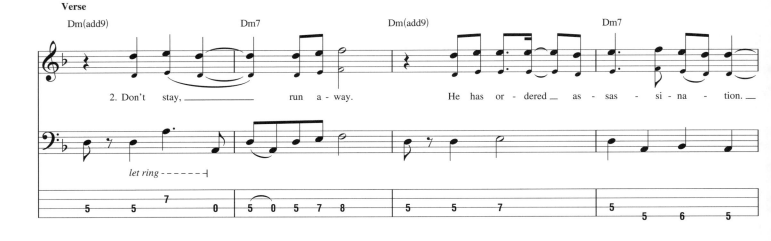

2. Don't stay, _____ run a-way. He has or-dered _ as-sas-si-na-tion. _

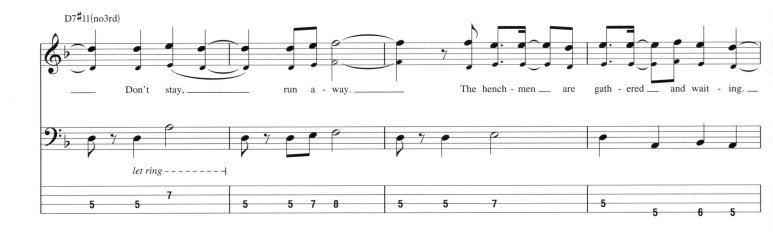

_____ Don't stay, _____ run a-way. _____ The hench-men _ are gath-ered _ and wait-ing. _

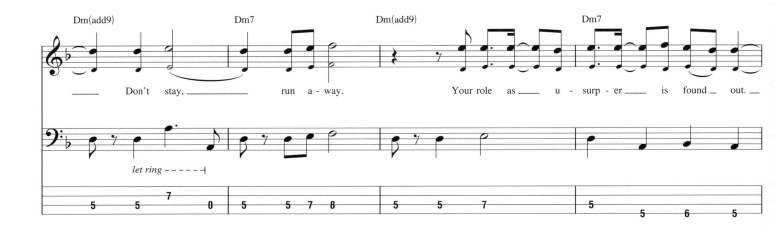

_____ Don't stay, _____ run a-way. Your role as _ u-surp-er _____ is found _ out.

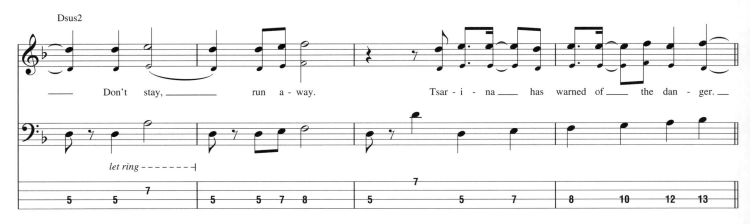

_____ Don't stay, _____ run a-way. Tsar-i-na _____ has warned of _____ the dan-ger.

Chorus

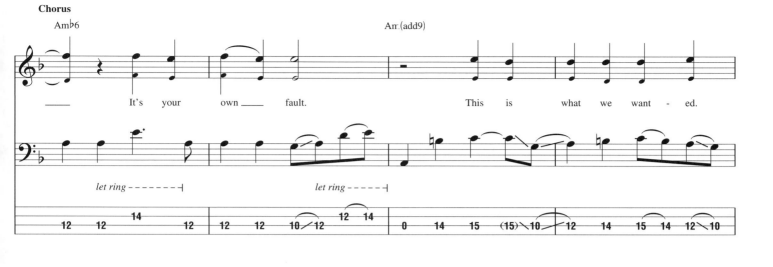

It's your own ___ fault. *This is what we want- ed.*

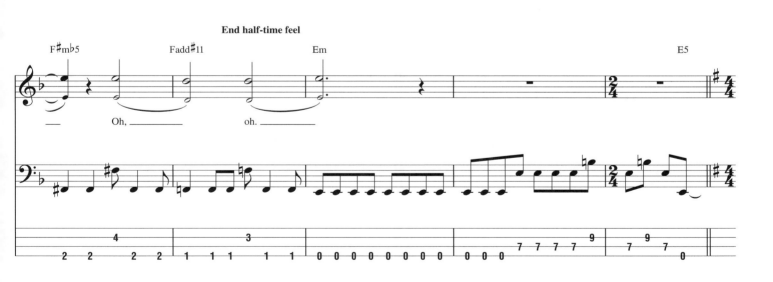

It's your own ___ fault. *This is where we lay. ___*

End half-time feel

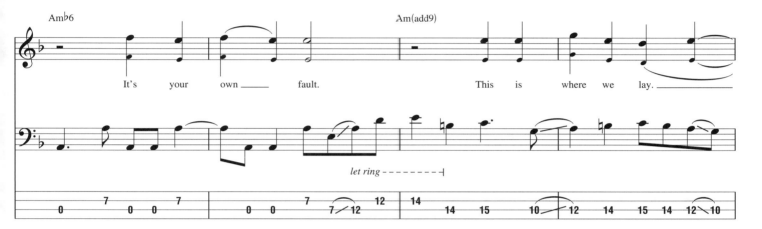

___ Oh, ___ oh. ___

"Escape"
Interlude

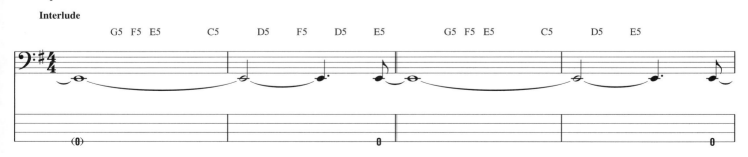

Chorus

the tides of blood,... Beau-ty's sud - den hand,... shat-tered crown.

(il - lu - mi - na - tion.

To Coda ⊕

Stretch-ing arms up high,... Leave the tsar to die.

we're on our way now.)

Interlude

(Ah, oo. Ah.)

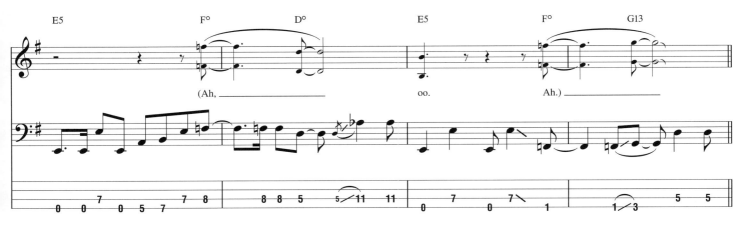

(Ah, oo. Ah.)

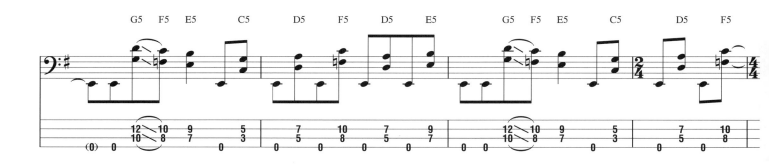

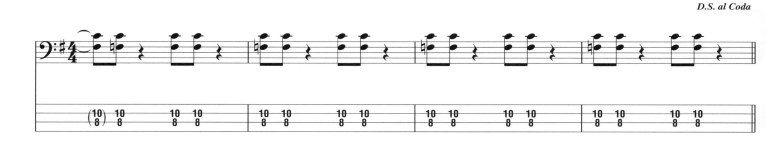

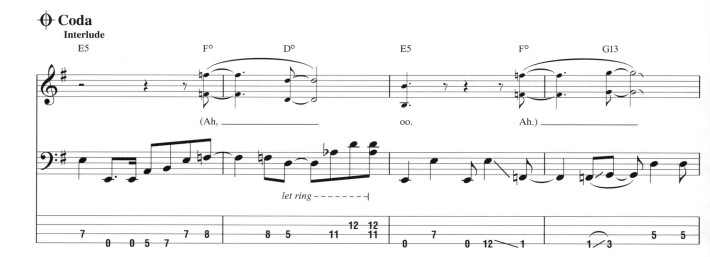

32

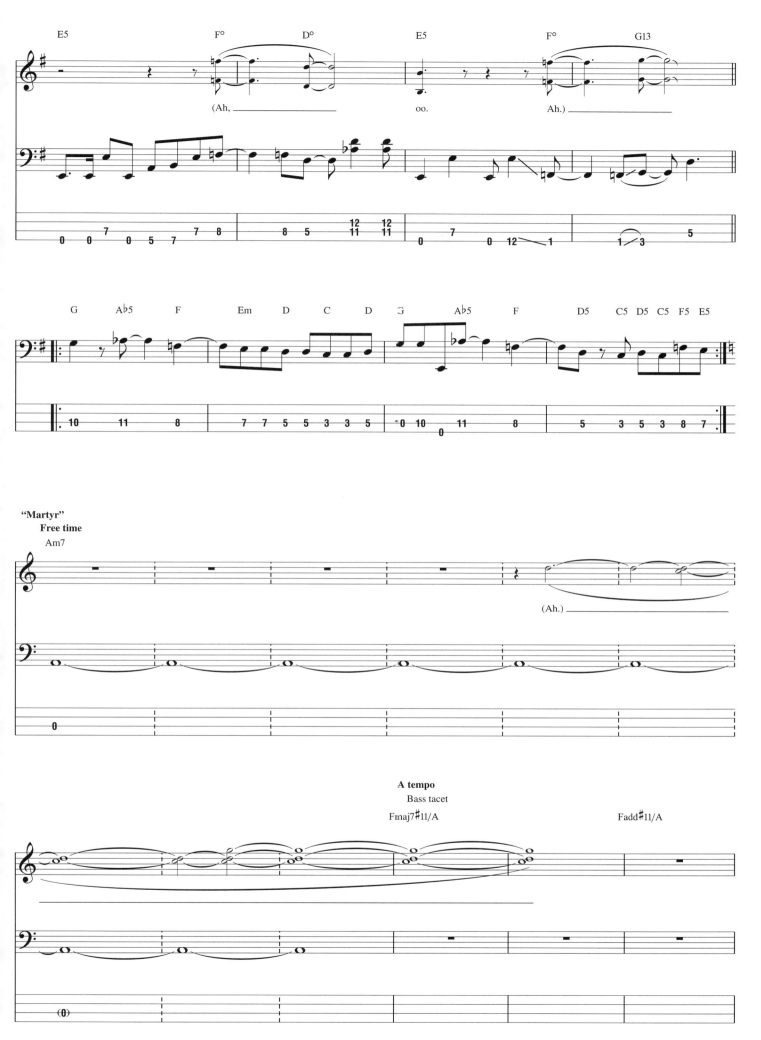

"Martyr"

Free time

A tempo
Bass tacet

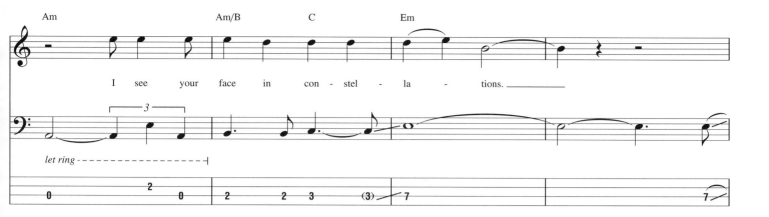

I see your face in con - stel - la - tions. _____

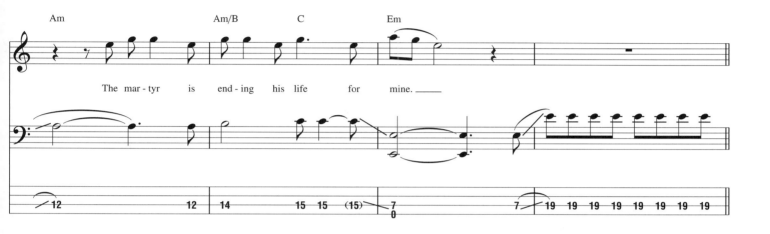

The mar - tyr is end - ing his life for mine. _____

Guitar Solo

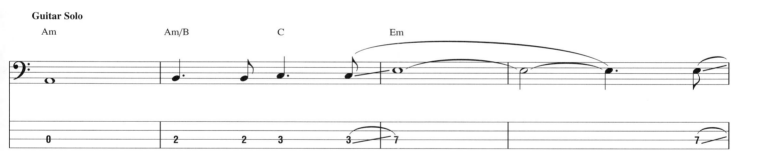

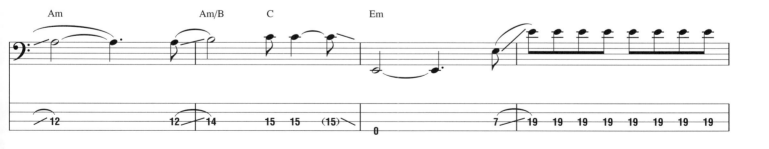

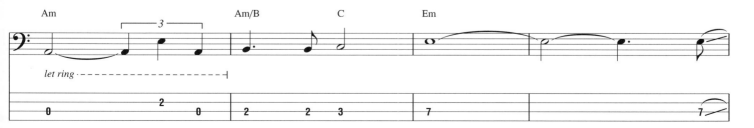

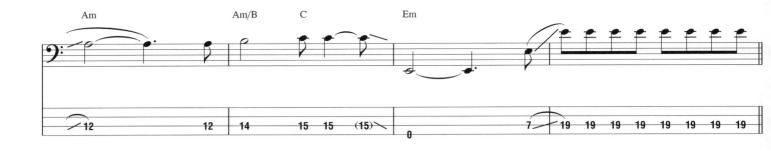

Interlude

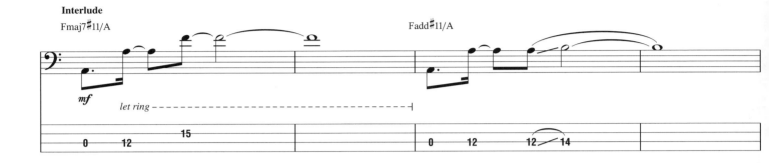

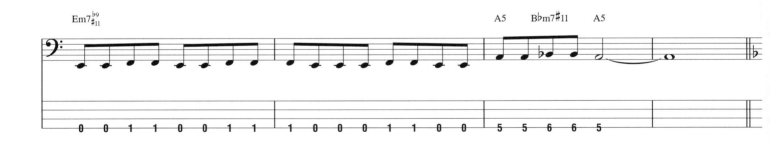

"Spiral"

Verse

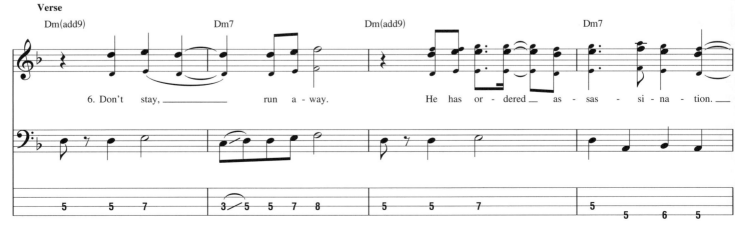

6. Don't stay, _____ run a - way. He has or - dered __ as - sas - si - na - tion.

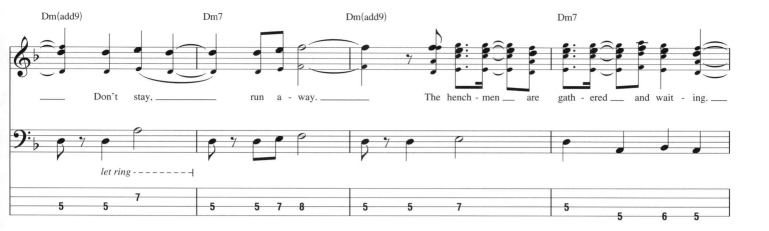

Don't stay, _____ run a-way. _____ The hench-men _____ are gath-ered _____ and wait- ing. _____

let ring - - - - - - - - -

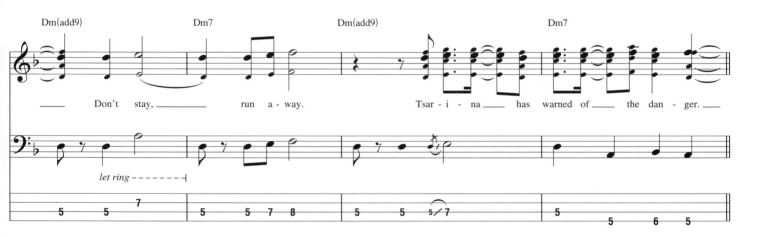

Don't stay, _____ run a-way. _____ Your role as _____ u - surp - er _____ is found out. _____

let ring - - - - - - -

Don't stay, _____ run a-way. _____ Tsar - i - na _____ has warned of _____ the dan - ger. _____

let ring - - - - - -

Interlude

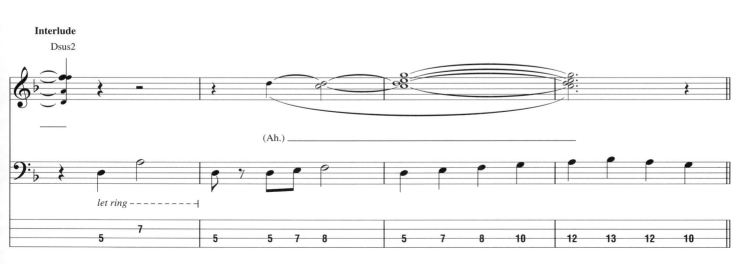

(Ah.) _____

let ring - - - - - - - - -

Chorus

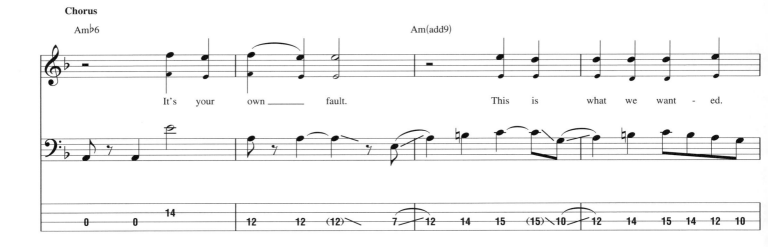

It's your own _____ fault. This is what we want - ed.

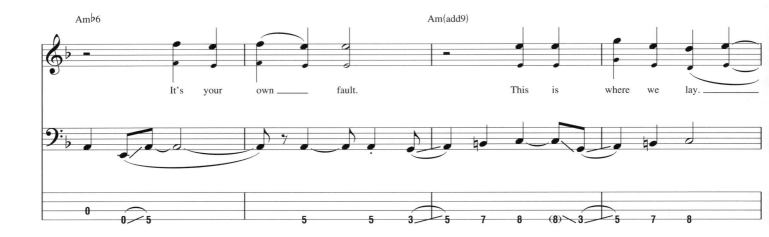

It's your own _____ fault. This is where we lay. _____

End half-time feel

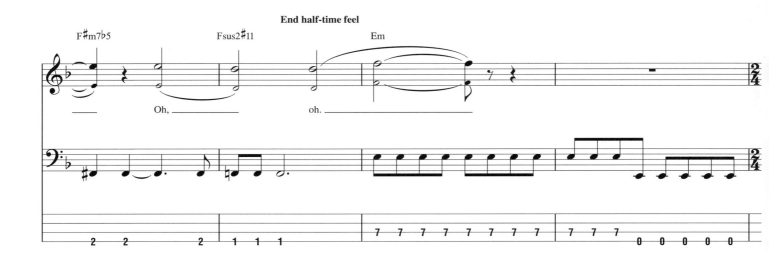

Oh, _____ oh. _____

Outro
Free time

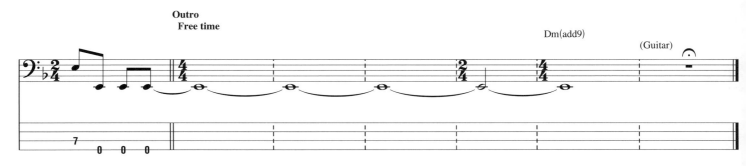

(Guitar)

Ghost of Karelia

Words and Music by Brann Dailor, William Hinds, William Kelliher and Troy Sanders

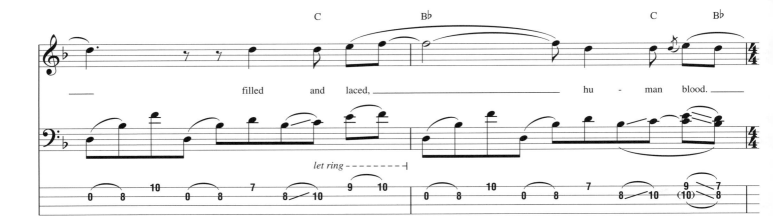

filled   and   laced, _____   hu - man   blood. _____

let ring ------------|

To Coda 2 ⊕

Interlude

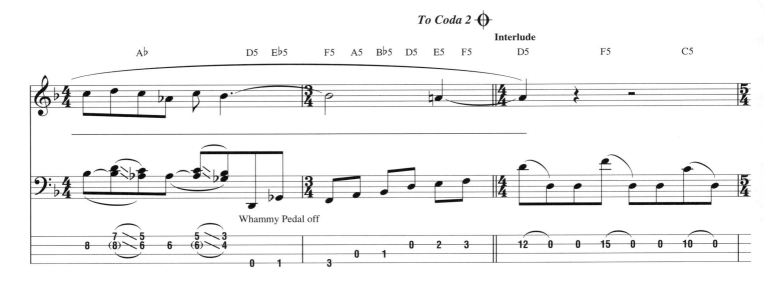

Whammy Pedal off

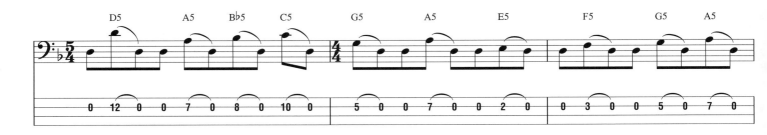

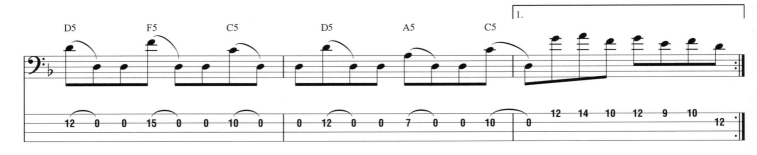

1.

2.

40

Chorus

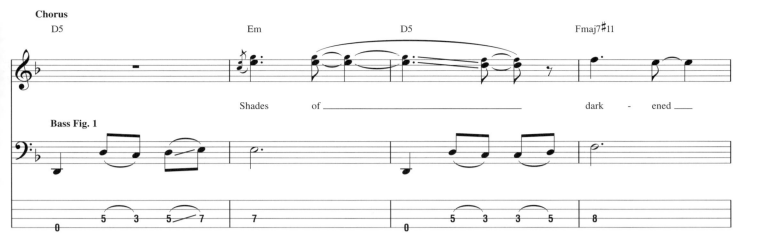

Shades of _____ dark - ened _____

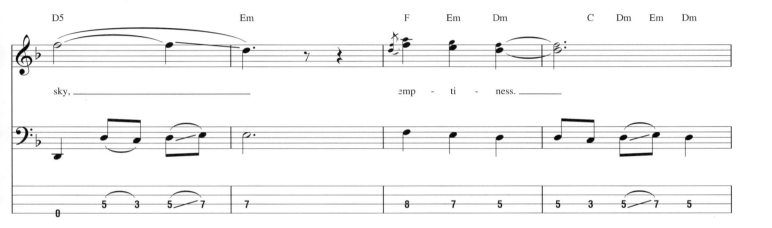

sky, _____ _____ emp - ti - ness. _____

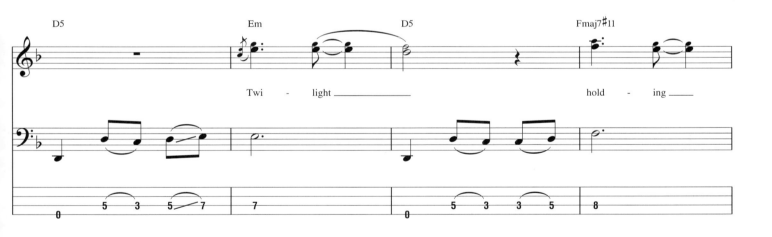

Twi - light _____ hold - ing _____

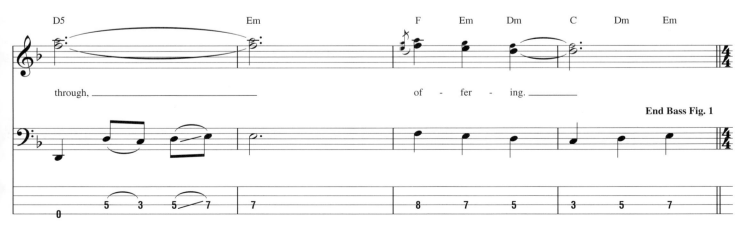

through, _____ of - fer - ing. _____

End Bass Fig. 1

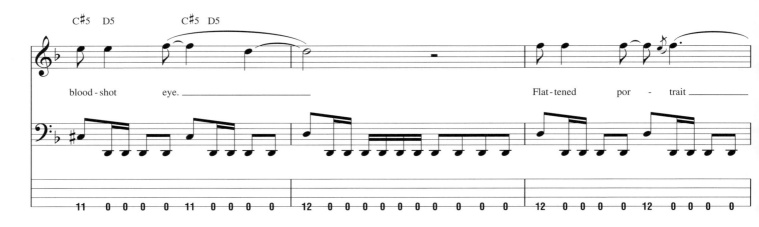

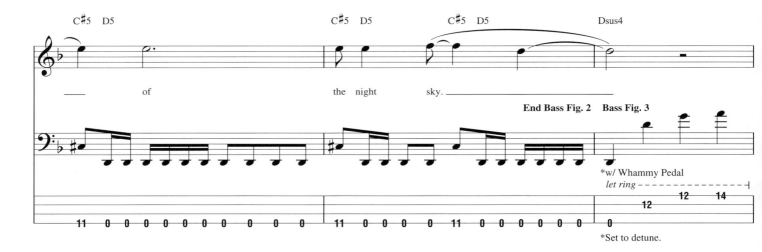

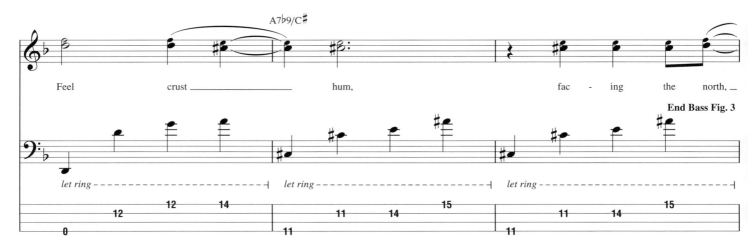

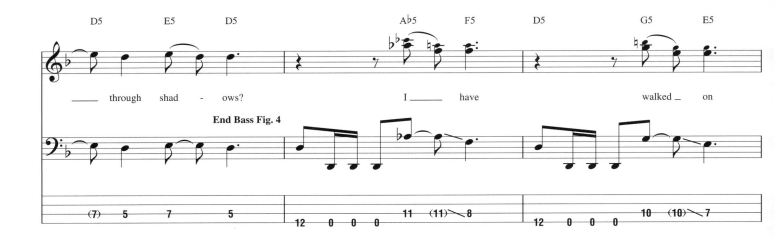

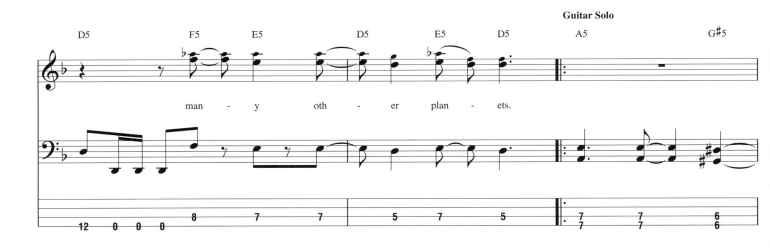

Guitar Solo

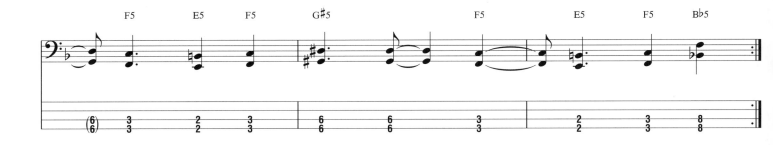

Bridge

Bass: w/ Bass Fig. 4 (2 times)

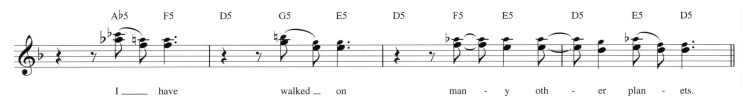

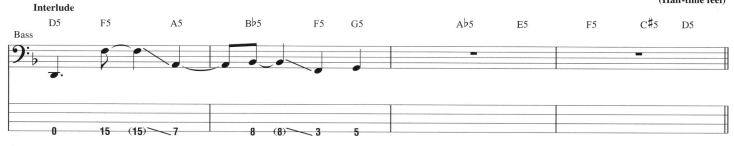

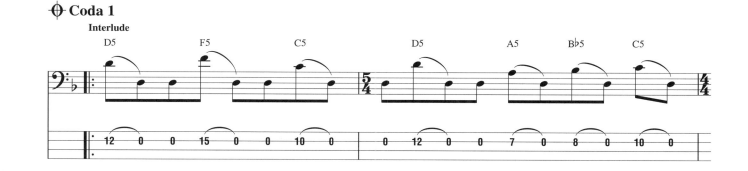

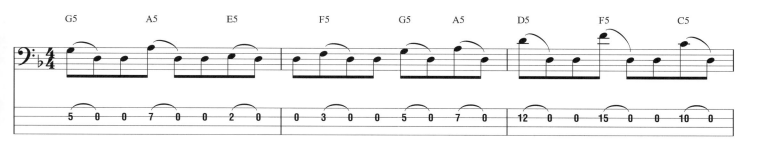

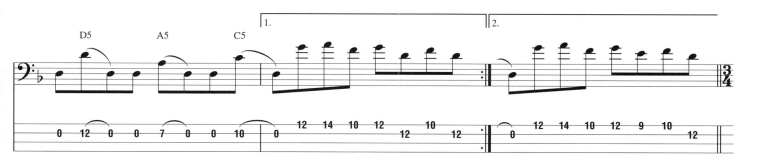

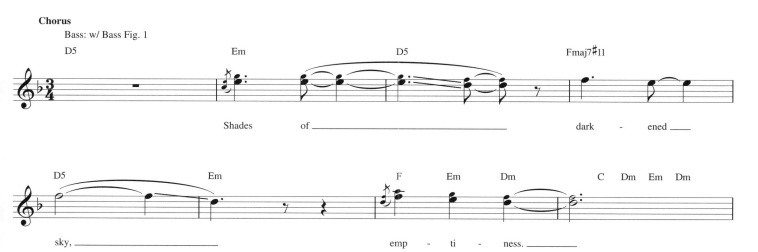

*Doubled by Moog Taurus Bass Pedal.

Crack the Skye

Words and Music by Brann Dailor, William Hinds, William Kelliher and Troy Sanders

Drop B tuning, down 1 step:
(low to high) A-G-C-F

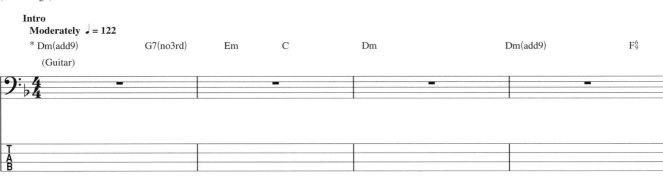

*Chord symbols reflect basic harmony.

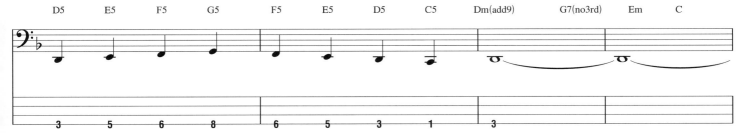

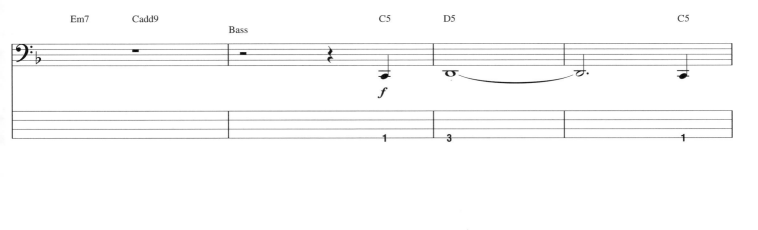

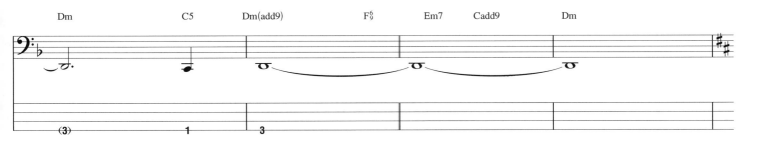

Guitar Solo

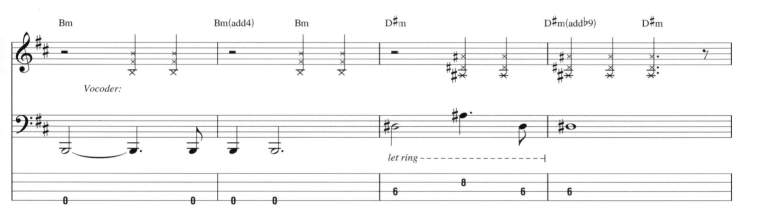

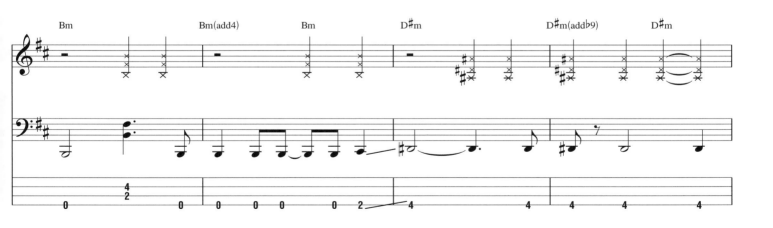

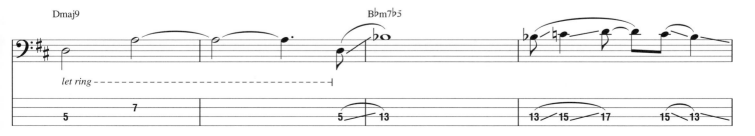

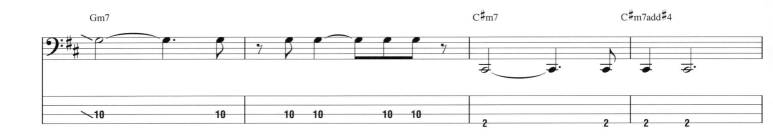

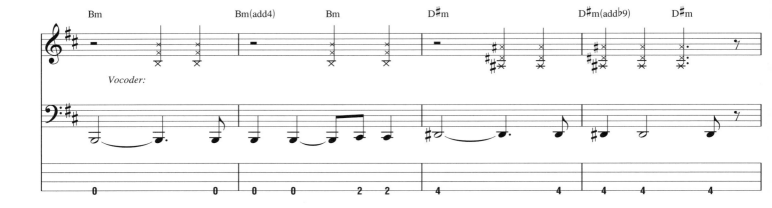

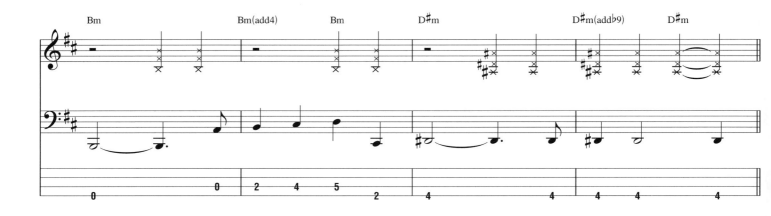

Interlude

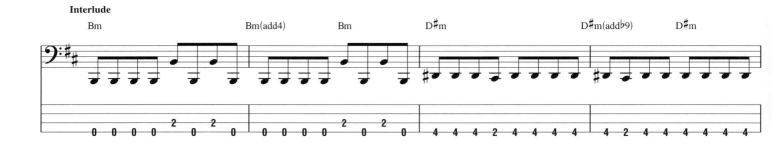

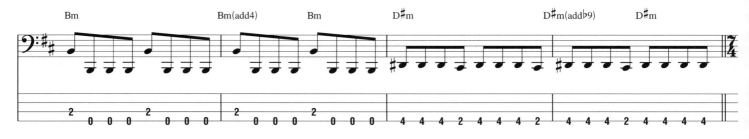

52

End half-time feel

B5 ... G

her _____ spir - it's too _____ strong. _____
(Strong.) _____

Chorus

Bass: w/ Bass Fig. 3 (2 times)

D#5 E5 F#5 G5 D#5   D   D#5 E5 F#5 G5   D#5   D

I   can   see   the   pain,   it's writ - ten all o - ver _____ your face. _____

D#5 E5 F#5 G5 D#5   D   D#5 E5 F#5 G5   D#5   D

_____ I   can   see   the   pain,   you can make _ it all go a - way.

Outro

Dm(add9)   G7(no3rd)   Em   C   Dm   C5   Dm(add9)   F⁶₉

Bass

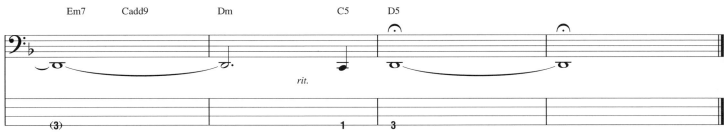

Em7   Cadd9   Dm   C5   D5

rit.

The Last Baron

Words and Music by Brann Dailor, William Hinds, William Kelliher and Troy Sanders

Drop D tuning, down 1 step:
(low to high) C-G-C-F

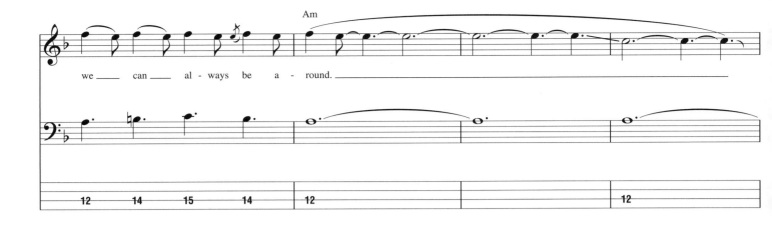

Verse
*Bass: w/ Bass Fig. 1 (1 1/2 times)

2. It is _____ hard _____ to see _____ through all ___ the haze ___ at ___ the
3. Fal - ter - ing foot - steps, ___ dead end path, _____ all that ___ I need ___ is _____ this

*w/ Whammy Pedal, set to detune.

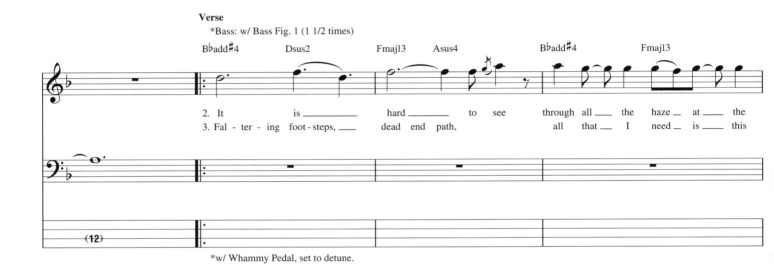

top ___ of ___ the trees. ___ I'll hold _____ my head _____ on sta - ble ground, ___
wise man's staff. ___ En - cased ___ in crys - tal, ___ he leads _____ the way. ___

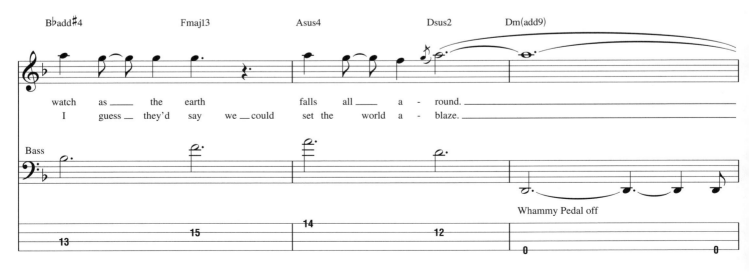

watch as ___ the earth falls all ___ a - round. _____
I guess ___ they'd say we ___ could set the world a - blaze. _____

Whammy Pedal off

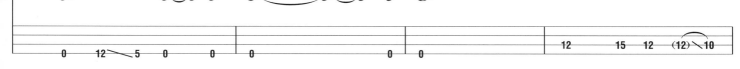

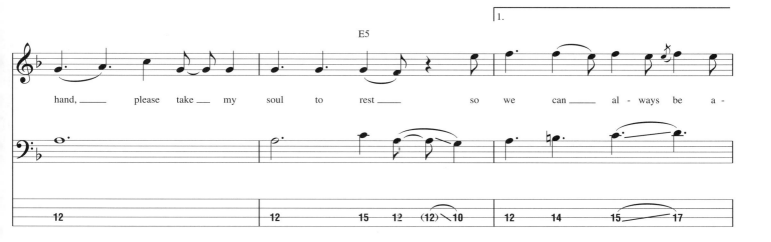

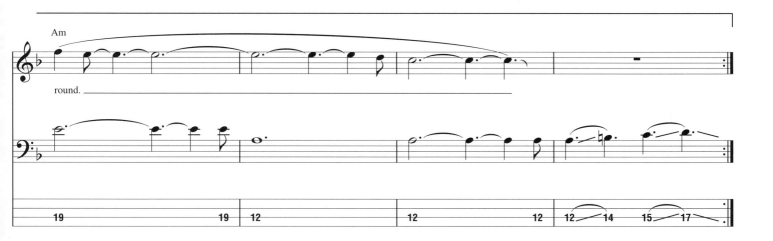

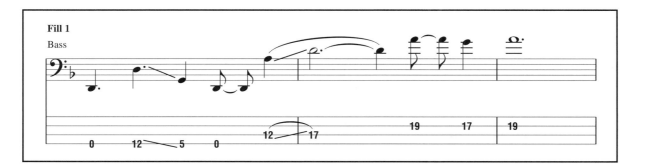

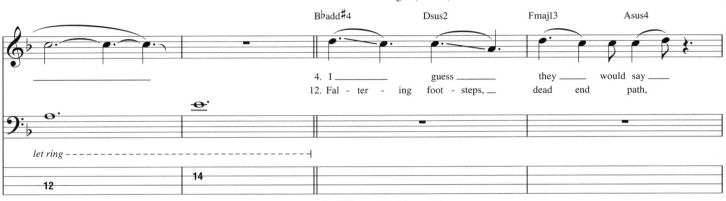

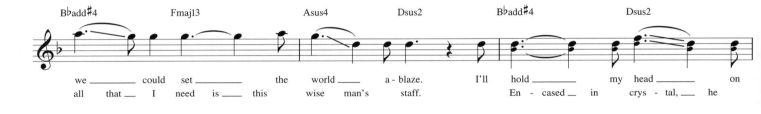

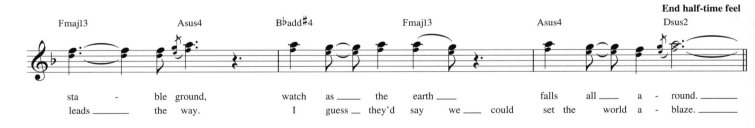

58

Verse

Half-time feel

5. Take my ____ black soul, a - live in ____ the fi - res ____ that burn ____ my skin. ____ Guide my eyes ____ all

*w/ Whammy Pedal, set to detune.

through ____ this maze, I ____ guess ____ they say ____ we could set the world ____ a - blaze. ____

Interlude

Yeah. ____ Yeah.

(Yeah.)

Slower ♩ = 92

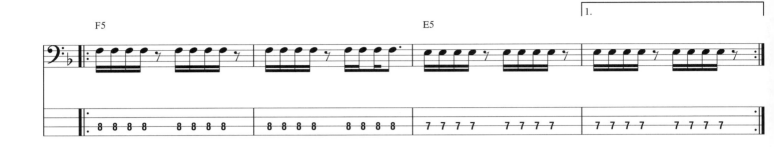

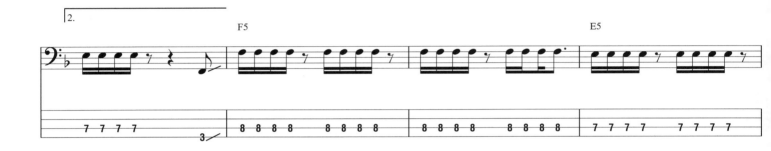

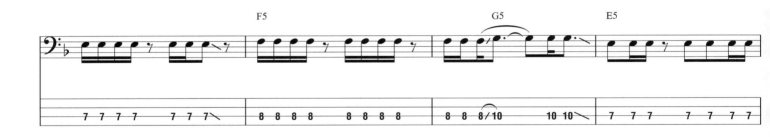

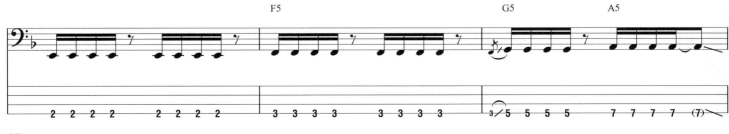

6., 8. All ___ that ___ I have seen, _____

stand - ing ___ on the edge, ___ foot of ___ prec - i - pice. _____

Float - ing ___ in the sea _____

past the ___ king of swords, quick - ly ___ to the shore. _____

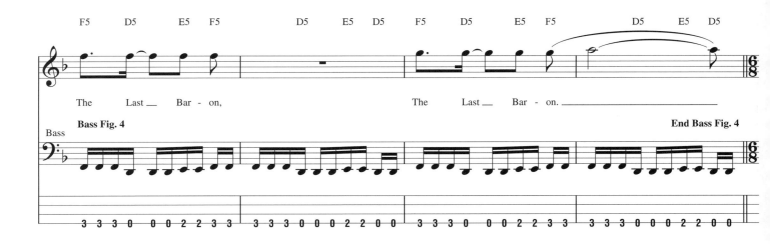

The   Last   Bar - on,   The   Last   Bar - on.

Chorus

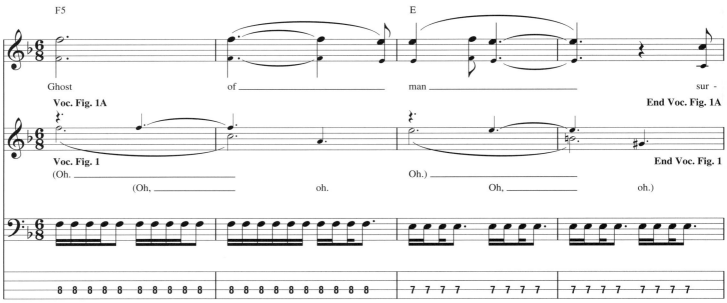

Ghost   of   man   sur -

(Oh.   Oh.)

(Oh,   oh.   Oh,   oh.)

Bkgd. Voc.: w/ Voc. Figs. 1 & 1A (3 times)   2nd time, Bass: w/ Fill 2

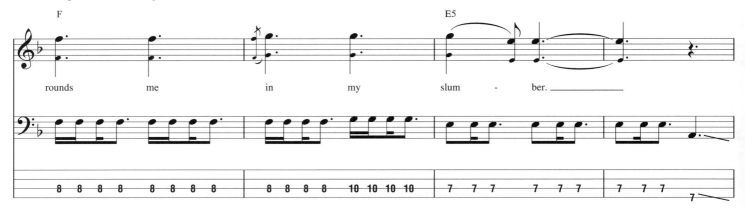

rounds   me   in   my   slum -   ber.

Fill 2

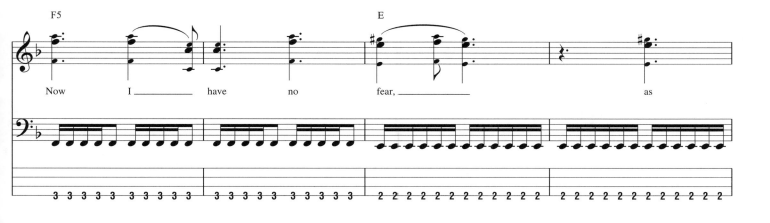

Now I _____ have no fear, _____ as

your wing is my shel - ter. _____

Verse

Bass tacet
Bass: w/ Bass Fig. 3 (2 times)

7., 9. Cy - a - nide he craves, _____

cours - ing _____ through his veins _____ pro - vid - ing _____ him with

strength. _____ See this _____ to the end, _____ a -

fraid of _____ psy - chic eyes, _____ faith in _____ mys - tic pow - er. _____

and I can't see _____ it.

End Bass Fig. 8

Bass: w/ Bass Fig. 8

And I was stand-ing, star-ing at the world _____ and I can't see __ it. __

Interlude

fuzz off

Bridge

*Bass: w/ Bass Fig. 8 (1 3/4 times)

D5 Eb5 C5 D5 F5   E5 C5 D5 C5 D5 E5 C5   D5 Eb5 C5 D5 F5 G5 A5 C5 A5 E5 F5 D5

And now I'm stand-ing, star-ing at the world _____ and I still can't see __ it. ___

*w/ fuzz

Eb5 C5 D5 F5   E5 C5 D5 C5 D5 E5 C5   D5 Eb5 C5 D5 F5

And now I'm stand - ing, star - ing at the world _____ and I

Interlude

Bass: w/ Bass Fig. 6

G5 A5 C5 A5 E5 F5 G5/D F#5/C# Eb5/Bb D5/A Eb5/Bb F#5/C#

still can't see it. _____

Bass

G5/D F#5/C# Eb5/Bb D5/A   G5/D F#5/C# Eb5/Bb D5/A Eb5/Bb F#5/C#

F#5   G5/D F#5/C# Eb5/Bb D5/A Eb5/Bb F#5/C#

G5/D F#5/C# Eb5/Bb D5/A   G5/D F#5/C# Eb5/Bb D5/A Eb5/Bb F#5/C#

And I was stand-ing, star-ing at the world, _____ I still can't see _____ it. _____

And I was stand ing, star-ing at the world _____ and I still can't see _____ it.

⊕ Coda 1

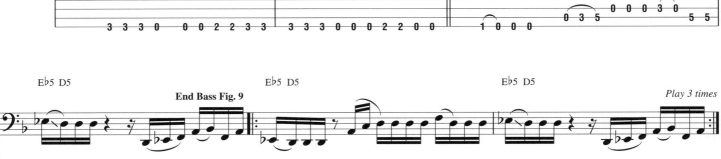

The Last _____ Bar - on. _____

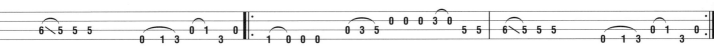

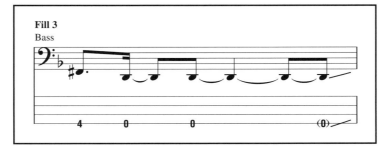

Chorus

Interlude

Bass: w/ Bass Fig. 9 (4 times)

Chorus

Bass: w/ Bass Fig. 5 (1 1/2 times)

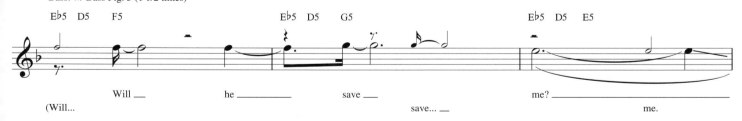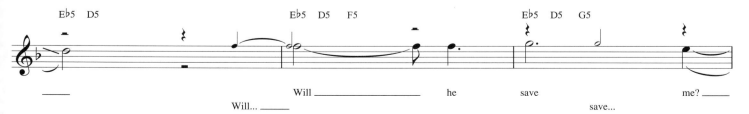

2nd time, Bass: w/ Fill 4   2nd time, Bass: w/ Fill 5

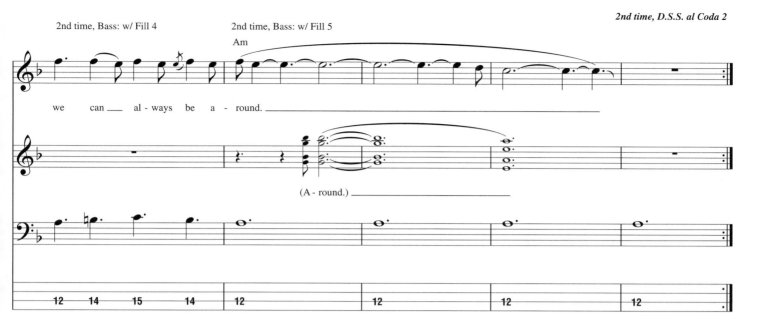

we   can ___ al - ways   be   a - round. _____

(A - round.) _____

Coda 2

Outro-Guitar Solo

Bass: w/ Bass Fig. 2 (8 times)

D5   C   D5   F5   E5

Play 8 times

D5   C   D5

Bass

F5   E5   N.C.

(Piano & sound effects)

17 sec.

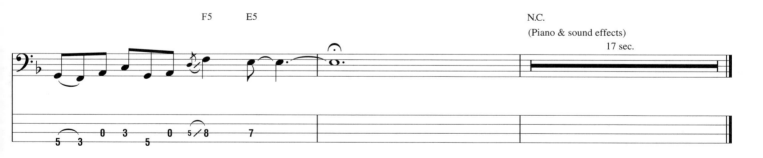

Fill 4

Bass

Fill 5

Bass

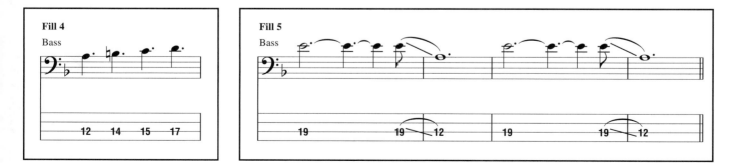

BASS RECORDED VERSIONS

Bass Recorded Versions® feature authentic transcriptions written in standard notation and tablature for bass guitar. This series features complete bass lines from the classics to contemporary superstars.

25 All-Time Rock Bass Classics
00690445 / $14.95

25 Essential Rock Bass Classics
00690210 / $15.95

Aerosmith Bass Collection
00690413 / $17.95

Best of Victor Bailey
00690718 / $19.95

Bass Tab 1990-1999
00690400 / $16.95

Bass Tab 1999-2000
00690404 / $14.95

Bass Tab White Pages
00690508 / $29.95

The Beatles Bass Lines
00690170 / $14.95

The Beatles 1962-1966
00690556 / $18.99

The Beatles 1967-1970
00690557 / $18.99

Best Bass Rock Hits
00694803 / $12.95

**Black Sabbath –
We Sold Our Soul For Rock 'N' Roll**
00660116 / $17.95

The Best of Blink 182
00690549 / $18.95

Blues Bass Classics
00690291 / $14.95

Boston Bass Collection
00690935 / $19.95

Chart Hits for Bass
00690729 / $14.95

The Best of Eric Clapton
00660187 / $19.95

Stanley Clarke Collection
00672307 / $19.95

Funk Bass Bible
00690744 / $19.95

Hard Rock Bass Bible
00690746 / $17.95

**Jimi Hendrix –
Are You Experienced?**
00690371 / $17.95

The Buddy Holly Bass Book
00660132 / $12.95

Incubus – Morning View
00690639 / $17.95

Iron Maiden Bass Anthology
00690867 / $22.99

Best of Kiss for Bass
00690080 / $19.95

Bob Marley Bass Collection
00690568 / $19.95

Best of Marcus Miller
00690811 / $19.99

Motown Bass Classics
00690253 / $14.95

Mudvayne – Lost & Found
00690798 / $19.95

Nirvana Bass Collection
00690066 / $19.95

No Doubt – Tragic Kingdom
00120112 / $22.95

The Offspring – Greatest Hits
00690809 / $17.95

**Jaco Pastorius –
Greatest Jazz Fusion Bass Player**
00690421 / $17.95

The Essential Jaco Pastorius
00690420 / $18.95

Pearl Jam – Ten
00694882 / $14.95

Pink Floyd – Dark Side of the Moon
00660172 / $14.95

The Best of Police
00660207 / $14.95

Pop/Rock Bass Bible
00690747 / $17.95

Queen – The Bass Collection
00690065 / $17.95

R&B Bass Bible
00690745 / $17.95

Rage Against the Machine
00690248 / $16.95

The Best of Red Hot Chili Peppers
00695285 / $24.95

**Red Hot Chili Peppers –
Blood Sugar Sex Magik**
00690064 / $19.95

**Red Hot Chili Peppers –
By the Way**
00690585 / $19.95

**Red Hot Chili Peppers –
Californication**
00690390 / $19.95

**Red Hot Chili Peppers –
Greatest Hits**
00690675 / $18.95

**Red Hot Chili Peppers –
One Hot Minute**
00690091 / $18.95

**Red Hot Chili Peppers –
Stadium Arcadium**
00690853 / $24.95

**Red Hot Chili Peppers –
Stadium Arcadium: Deluxe Edition**
Book/2-CD Pack
00690863 / $39.95

Rock Bass Bible
00690446 / $19.95

Rolling Stones
00690256 / $16.95

System of a Down – Toxicity
00690592 / $19.95

Top Hits for Bass
00690677 / $14.95

**Stevie Ray Vaughan –
Lightnin' Blues 1983-1987**
00694778 / $19.95

0309